THERE IS A CURSE IN THIS HOUSE

WHO BROUGHT IT?

Kwabena Quayson

Title: *There is a Curse in this house*
          Who brought it?

Author: Kwabena Quayson
Copyright © 2019

First print

Produced by Galilee
www.galilee.com
Cover/Interior design: Galilee

All scriptures are from the King James version or New King James version, unless otherwise stated.

Royal Library reg.nr: 020-14249
ISBN: 978-9493105-18-8

CONTENT

“Our fathers have sinned,
and are not; and we have
borne their iniquities.”

Lamentations 5:7

"If you ignore your family history, you will repeat it...."

Bishop Dr. Abraham Chigbundu

Dedication

I dedicate this book to my son, Emmanuel Quayson - Quayson. You have been through a lot but your challenges continue to inspire me to trust the Lord through it all. I know your deliverance is here. And to my entire beautiful family for what we have been through... surely the sound of the abundant rain is nigh.

Acknowledgements

First and foremost I would like to thank God the Father. In the process of time, He has caused men to ride upon our heads, brought us through fire and waters to a place of glory. He has put the pieces of our lives together and revealed mysteries to us. I could never have done this without His guidance. To God Almighty be all the glory.

I can barely find the words to express all the wisdom, love and support I have enjoyed from these abled people of God in my (spiritual) journey: My Archbishop Dr. Akwasi Asare Bediako, Rev. Owusu Richard, Bishop Yaw Owusu Ansah, Apostle Livingstone Kofi Tsagli, all of Resurrection Power and Living Bread Ministries Int. Rev. Dr. Tom Marfo, Rev. Eastwood Anaba, Bishop Agyenasare, Apostle General Korankye - Ankrah and Elder Frank Donkor, of Hebron Prayer Camp. To you all, I am deeply and sincerely grateful.

I have enjoyed numerous supports through inputs, feedbacks and encouragements from some great and anointed people of God during the writing of this book: first to my understanding wife Mrs. Christie (Alberta)

Quayson, what can I say? You are one of the main reasons that I am still standing. I am so thankful that I have you in my corner pushing me when I am ready to give up. Thanks for not just believing, but knowing that I could do this! Your godly counsel, prayers and ideas and more especially faith have been immeasurable. I Love you always and forever! To my children: you are the best gifts that I have ever had in my life! You give me something to live for. A better life for you than I had is all I want. I love you all more than you will ever know.

I am indebted to Rt. Rev. Dr. Nana Anyani–Boadum who wrote the foreword and Rev. Jones Owusu Adjei who took time to edit the manuscript. During this journey, I also enjoyed much love and emotional supports and prayers from a larger community: Apostle Kwadwo Amponsah Asare, and Frank Asirifi Bempong for his contribution to this project. To Prophet Charles Entsir- Eghan, Rev. Nelson Boateng Frimpong, Rev. Emmanuel Koney, Apostle Ernest Adeti and wife Bella, Apostle Jones Dada Boateng, Bishop Dr. Abraham Chigbundu, Rev. Sunshine Adams, Pastor Kingsley K. Yeboah and all my fellow workers of Ambushment Council Europe. To my Spiritual daughter, Deaconess Dr. (Mrs.) Joan Vondee-Awortwi, your earnest encouragement has made this project possible. I know God brought you into my life for you to help me in my ministry and truly, without you, I couldn't have written this book. You're blessed forever, Dr. Joan!

The last but not the least, I am grateful for my branch, Dominion Centre, The Hague, The Netherlands and the entire REPLIB body of Christ for their diverse supports rendered in various ways.

Foreword

Rt. Rev. Dr. Nana Anyani-Boadum

Let me quote from the first lines of Sophocles' Antigone, where the title character bemoans her fate to the chorus: How many miseries our father caused! And is there one of them that does not fall on us while yet we live?

Antigone must reckon with the choices her father Oedipus made and the slippery, obscure moral inheritance that he leaves her. She ultimately chooses to pay with her life, not for her sins, but for her father's.

Children reckoning with and re-enacting the sins of their forebears is a key part of the tragic form.

The author Quayson Kay's references to the theory of "path dependence" which suggest that "history matters in the first paragraph of chapter one is therefore very appropriate to the subject matter in this book on Curses.

Even though the media and the entertainment industry often portray a bizarre demonology and angelology alien to sound biblical narratives, there is enough biblical instances both in the Old and New Testament of the

Holy Bible that gives a strong theological stance on the reality of Curses. Curses can have a real effect on those who have not accepted Jesus Christ as their personal saviour. It is also very important to state that people who have noticed the deadly presence of ancestral curses in their bloodline should seek deliverance from their ancestral lineage even though they are Christians. The writer Quayson Kay has stressed on the point of seeking deliverance after salvation, and I must say that I identify with that position.

A curse is the opposite of a blessing. They are quite real. When Jesus cursed the fig tree, it was not without a very dramatic effect. The result evoked astonishment – as it indeed would if a curse runs through your family. But let me quickly state that in the realms of the spirit certain things are far beyond the possibility of what demons can do. It is God who judges people and decides on their eternal fate. Demons cannot just go on rampage kidnapping and destroying people's lives without a cause. For a curse therefore to have effect on any person or any group of people, there must be a cause, which renders the offender and possibly his descendants vulnerable to imprecation of divine punishment.

This is clearly enforced in Proverbs 26:2 *"Like a fluttering sparrow or a darting swallow, an undeserved curse will not land on its intended victim"* (NLT).

I entreat the reader to carefully read this book on curses by Rev. Quayson Kay as a mirror that will help you to identify the type of curse that is manifesting in your personal life or running through your family. Every one of us is connected to a family tree. None of us is a product of a cosmic accident. Our ancestral past is fraught with so much despicable deeds that may hunt our children and us if they are not dealt with by the washing of the blood of Jesus. We must therefore do all spiritual due-diligence to save ourselves and the generation after us. Pastor Quayson Kay through this book offers us the opportunity to take the first step in bringing deliverance to our family.

You cannot choose your relatives any more than you can choose skin colour, gender, or race. Someone up the family tree could be the cause of a generational curse, because he or she left the family front door open for Satan and his cohorts to enter.

It might be that the generational bondage your family is going through is a result of a heinous crime or sin by an ancestor perpetrated against some innocent people who in return imposed a curse on your family.

The effect of such curses is often seen by the sin patterns, sicknesses, and the hardships that repeat themselves from generation to generation. It is not uncommon to see a particular sickness or disease run through a family without any Pathological conditions, signs and symptoms of any abnormal anatomical or physiological conditions. It is also not uncommon to see rejection, sexual sins and perversions, aberrant religious beliefs, witchcraft, and rebellion in a single family. Demons often claim the bloodline of families where curses exist and use that as access to the entire family. The bible says in Ezekiel 18:2 *"The fathers have eaten sour grapes, and the children's teeth are set on edge?"*

The effect of this parable is what Reverend Quayson Kay is seeking to undo in this book as he carefully helps to walk you through various types of curses and how to seek deliverance.

I've watched Quayson Kay growing up in the Christian faith and have always admired his quest for the truth, his zeal for righteous living and his desire to reach out to those outside the church is highly commendable. I'm therefore not surprised that Quayson Kay has spent time to research into the subject of curses in order to bring deliverance to those in bondage and bring them to the saving-knowledge of Christ Jesus.

I urge whoever is holding this book to make time to read. Maybe you have unconsciously become a victim of the "myth" which says, "I don't have time". That is why I said though you may not have the time "Make time" to read this book on curses. It will do you and the generation after you lots of good.

Quayson Kay, my prayer for you is in Isaiah 50:4. May God give you the tongue of the learned.

"The Lord GOD hath given me the tongue of the learned, that I should know how to speak a word in season to him that is weary: he wakeneth morning by morning, he wakeneth mine ear to hear as the learned".

May God bless the work of your hands. Psalm 90:17
"And let the beauty of the Lord our God be upon us: and establish thou the work of our hands upon us; yea, the work of our hands establish thou it".

Congratulations Quayson Kay.

Apostle Jones Owusu Adjei

A good writing piece that interrogates and explain demonic influences on people as a result of their personal, communal or ancestral engagement with divine abominations.

I like how your arguments are put forward. It challenges, "Once born again, forever free from generational/ancestral curses" believers to rethink their position.

Chapter 1
Introduction

Everybody would be willing to admit that most of the things individuals do have durable consequences. In social sciences there is a concept or theory called **path dependence**, based on a straightforward assumption that *"history matters or we are where we are today because of what happened in the past."* This concept or theory attempts to explain exactly how history matters through the studies of the means by which restrictions on normal behaviour become committed to develop in certain ways as a result of structural properties or beliefs and values. This can be minor, momentary advantage or a seemingly inconsequential act, behaviour, decision or standard but can have important and irreversible influences on the lives of majority of people and situations for a long period of time.

History therefore plays a very important role in our lives. As we inquire, we acquire knowledge on events of the past to help us examine and analyse a sequence of past events, and to objectively determine the patterns of cause and effect that determine them today. However, the tendency of a past to continue even if better options or alternatives are available depends on how one would want to exercise free will and the illumination one receives.

This would mean that, our current situation might not necessarily be as a result of our own actions. However, whatever decision or path we choose to tread today may affect not only us (today) but also the future of many to come.

What I am drawing our attention to, is the fact that a lot had gone on way before we were born (and some of us witnessed some acts as we grew up) and to a large extent these acts have shaped or influenced our lives and if allowed, may continue despite the many other alternatives available. I promise readers- by the time you finish reading this book, not only would you have known about your background, but would have been enlightened and empowered to break and depart from any unfruitful path and cycle or occurrences and would have found out a lot more than just looking on and living unfruitful life despite the many efforts and hard works.

When I was growing up, I saw images of wild animals strategically inscribed right in the open space of our family house and blood sacrifices were made often on those animal images. I remember how on every Friday, sheep and dogs would be slaughtered and schnapps (Hard Liquor) poured on the images and incantations made. Afterwards, the meat would then be shared among family members for their weekend meals. To the family it was enjoyment time and therefore least thought of the effects of these on themselves, their children, grandchildren and the unborn generation. Occasionally, the slaughtering were done for and on behalf of the general public who sometimes came to admire, get some meat for their meals (probably because they could not afford to buy), or to join in petitioning of prayers offered for protection and help. Drumming with women singing spiritual songs for a fetish priest dressed in his war-like clothes to dance around and perform some rituals that were believed to have brought healings and other prosperities followed the evenings of such days. The whole family embraced these practices and followed the head of the family (my grandfather) who authorised the acts thereby making it a perpetuated family shrine.

From all indications, I come from an idolatrous family where no records were kept as to when it all started but oral history confirmed my grandfather bringing a god called *"Tigari"* into the family from a town in the northern part of Ashanti Region called *Faamang*. No reasons were given as to why that particular god. Probably, as the family head, he had sought it as protection for himself and his nuclear family, which later turned to be a family property after his death. No one ever asked or thought of the effects and implications (if any), were on the family after that generation was over. For me this was a question that needed an answer because as I became a bible believer, one of the first things I learnt was how Jehovah God hates idol worshipping. The punishment of which extends to generations yet unborn. Many people and readers may identify with this situation or similar acts.

The family head died in 1968. Surprisingly, after his death, it became difficult getting a successor for the shrine! None of his successors was prepared to serve the shrine; nothing was known with regards to requirements and therefore it was abandoned for years. Many attempts were made to no avail regarding what to do with the *gods*. Every decision was inconclusive; some family members who were Christians at that time wanted the entities burnt whilst others vehemently objected to the idea. Finally, in 2006, a consensus was reached to return the entities to their owners in the Northern part of Ashanti Region. This was greatly influenced by the new family head who was young and an Apostle of the Gospel. A delegation was sent to inform the *chief owners* of the family's decision to return the gods to them. The owners gave conditions to meet before accepting the gods back; blood sacrifices were required on that date! Our family agreed to that and so in August 2006, a powerful delegation led by the Chief Linguist of the Asamankese Chieftaincy returned the *gods* to their original owners! The owners made for and on behalf of the family sacrifices and the gods were taken back!

Life took a different turn for us after the gods were sent back. I will say with all certainty without doubt those cursed objects left a bloodline pattern I call a curse in our home. It is very difficult to explain but the surviving elders gave history of how the family was before the introduction of those objects. Marriage became an issue; those already in were getting divorced whilst those yet to be were not getting any and so women were growing into their late ages without getting married, men were sleeping around; education no more became important and even those already in school were dropping out either for lost of interest or poor performances, the issue of non-accomplishment surfaced. Those in businesses began to experience loss and incurred debts; strange sickness and diseases were to say the least that happened. All these mishaps became the order of the day due to the adoption of the idolatry practices. It did not happen one time to particular people; neither did it happen for a while. It became a *legacy* passed on from descendants to descendants and unto the next.

Nonetheless, the bible makes it clear in Hebrews 9:17 *"For a testament is of force after men are dead: otherwise it is of no strength at all while the testator liveth"*. This scripture opened my mind up into thinking a wrong agreement was made and its time bound was after the death of my grandfather.

Everybody either experienced one or all. If you have ever been to the hospital and the doctors asked you- do you have this or that (in relation to a particular genetic sickness or disease) in your family then you would understand what I mean by it becoming a path or legacy.

I say with all certainty that most if not all mishaps and evil occurrences in the house had been as a result of my grandfather's acts! Though I cannot sincerely tell of the options that were available to him, one can only say it was the price he paid to enter into that covenant perhaps, for his momentary personal interest. He committed an abomination before God. He transgressed against the first commandment: *"And God spoke all these words, saying, I am the Lord thy God, which have brought thee out of the land of Egypt, out of the house of bondage. Thou shalt have no other gods before me."* (Exodus 20:1-3)

After I accepted Jesus Christ as my personal Savior, my favourite scripture was **2 Corinthians 5:17** *"therefore if any man be in Christ, he is a new creature: old things are passed away; behold, all things are become new."* I had thought that the death and resurrection of my Lord Jesus Christ had dealt with my past and the blood He shared had wiped out every unpleasant situation in my life. But it was not so! I suffered what has become legacy in my father's house in every aspect of my life. I prayed and quoted scriptures and did what I was *supposed* to do as a born again in Christ but nothing seemed to have changed if not worsened. We will go into scriptures to enlighten ourselves to help us know that despite the many packages our Lord Jesus has provided, it is up to us to deal with every unpleasant background or situation or root cause in our lives using the authority He has given us.

Whether you will agree with me or you will argue with me, there is a root cause to every situation and it affects any human being born of a woman. Even medical science tries to find causes to every sickness that is why genes and medical records are very important to doctors and specialists. If we agree with medical science that people inherit sickness and other genetics issues (height, weight, complexion, etc. etc.), why can't we accept that people can also inherit curses or blessings? If you are fortunate to have come from a godly home where forefathers believed

God, lived and walked according to His laws and statues, you are blessed! But even that, continue to search and deliver yourself and the next generation because some root causes are time bound! It can be a blessing or it can be a curse. But if your life is such that you can take a minute and glance through your family line and confirm a particular pattern for a long period, then come with me as we unravel the puzzle: there is a curse in this house to find out what it is, who brought it and how to deal with it.

Many of us have been born again, received Holy Spirit baptism and speak in tongues but are still suffering. Of course our Lord Jesus Christ did not promise us easy life on earth but surely He didn't promise us suffering. He said tribulation and persecution. We are not enjoying what we were made to enjoy simply because we have not received enough illumination and therefore misquote and misinterpret scriptures. It saddens my heart so much when I meet Christians who are of the view that there is no need for deliverance because the blood has bought us, we have been redeemed from every curse, we are in the era of dispensation of grace and so on and so forth, my heart bleeds for the lack of knowledge. In the subsequent chapters, we will look at mighty men in the bible such as Abraham, Isaac, Jacob, Moses, John the Baptist, Paul and others who were used mightily by God yet had their past (ancestral consequence or their own acts) still hanging and working against them. Their past, history or background cleaved unto them and worked against them. Believe me, it is not only in the Old Testament as people are quick to say; "Christ had not yet come and we were under the law and Hebrews 9[1] sums it all up for us ... Jesus has paid it all as the High Priest."

Indeed Jesus has done it all for us but it is up to us to activate and exercise authority. Of what use is it to you if you have the key to a house but stand in the rain or you having food but crying of hunger?

In our next chapter we will discuss what a curse is, types of curses and bring out some biblical examples. In Luke 8:10, our Lord Jesus Christ said *"unto you it is given to know the mysteries of the kingdom of God: but to others in parables; that seeing they might not see, and hearing they might not understand."* Glory is to the Father who through Christ has revealed the mysteries of the kingdom unto us. It is my prayer you would not be among the "others" who cannot see or understand what they hear.

---

[1] The high priest enters the Most Holy Place once a year with blood, Christ entered the true holy place once for all by His own blood. Paul emphasized in Hebrews Chapter 9 that Christ, the High Priest, was a perfect tabernacle. This was because He offered His own blood – blood without blemish – to save mankind. Therefore the sacrifice of Christ served to accomplish eternal redemption, cleansing of the conscience, redemption from curse and washing away of our sins. This means that, the wrongdoings under the first covenant (old testament) were cleansed once and for all.

Chapter 2

Dealing with Curses, Types of Curses with Biblical Examples

Many Christians do not believe that a Christian can be cursed nor do they understand what a curse really is.

A curse is a negative decree that is proclaimed upon either living or non-living things (human beings, animals, a place or location, environments, etc.) for either material, physical, emotional, psychological or spiritual destruction or even physical death.

Many writers and books classify curse into many types. But, however one looks at it, there is one comprehensive type of curse -*Personal Curse* that disintegrates into many branches of curses. In other words, every curse begins with a personal act that later becomes *Generational Curses* or whatever type one may define. These are actually occurrences of compelling habits, contrary behaviours or reoccurring calamities that seem to beset members of the family who are born to that specific bloodline. It can be rape, poverty, stealing, divorce, bareness, miscarriages, alcoholism, drug addiction, sexual affections, premature death, smoking, diseases and sickness etc. The agents of these are demons that are passed down through the transfer of blood and genetic information. This curse can be an addition code within the DNA strand or it could just be a demonic spirit that has attached itself to the DNA and manipulates the genetic information. This genetic information would then be demonic false information that would then be the blue print of the person or family's life.

A very critical look at the bible proves that all curses from God, the devil and man that became short lived or prolonged generation began with one personal or group of people's act. Examples from the bible include Gehazi in II Kings 5:27, Matthew 27:25 and in Genesis 49 as Jacob blessed and enforced the roots of his children's destinies. Each of his sons received according to their deeds, which later became the trends for their descendants and generations. The word **Generation(al)** came from the word **Gene**, which is the DNA material of all life force. So when the bible talks about generational curses, it is talking about curses that have been placed in the gene of a particular family bloodline. And how was it placed? Through an act! An act by one or more people! Family curses are reoccurring problems that steal, kill, and destroy. Ezekiel 16:44, *"Behold, every one that useth proverbs shall use this proverb against thee, saying, As is the mother, so is her daughter."* These are generational curses inherited from bloodline, passed on from parents to offspring.

A curse comes directly from source (the pronouncer) through sin or an open door. John 9:1-3

"And as Jesus passed by, he saw a man which was blind from his birth. And his disciples asked him, saying, Master, who did sin, this man, or his parents, that he was born blind? Jesus answered, Neither hath this man sinned, nor his parents: but that the works of God should be made manifest in him." From this scripture, it is obvious that the parents' sins could bring a family curse of blindness or the man himself.

As I said earlier, most curses are carried out by demons, and in most cases, the demons that carry the generation curses live inside the person! We must know however that, demons cannot enter a person until given legal right or open door! That is why Ecclesiastes 10:8, makes it clear that *"He that diggeth a pit shall fall into it; and whoso breaketh an hedge, a serpent shall bite him."* Demons need an entry point through sins or door opener to be able to get into a person's life. In the spirit world, there are spiritual laws and demons cannot violate these laws without severe consequences. Just as we must open our heart for Jesus Christ to come in, it is the same way a person must open his or herself up for demons to come in.

We cannot talk about curse and ignore its sources. Curses may come from God as a result of disobedience and may be accomplished by divine decree with no demonic interference, but most curses are accomplished by the operation of demons as the Lord allows. However, all curses through witchcraft (from the devil) are accomplished by demons.

Some people and Christians for that matter do not believe that Almighty God can curse a person but in Isaiah 34:5 God saying *"For my sword shall be bathed in heaven: behold, it shall come down upon Edom, and upon the people of my curse, to judgment."*
In the Bible, we see repeatedly where God placed generational curses on certain people. An example is David in 2 Samuel 12:10 *"Now therefore the sword shall never depart from thine house; because thou hast despised me, and hast taken the wife of Uriah the Hittite to be thy wife."*

If we believe God does not curse, then what do we make of Genesis 12:3, when He said *"And I will bless them that bless thee, and curse him that curseth thee: and in thee shall all families of the earth be blessed."* In Deuteronomy 28:45, God says, *"Moreover all these curses shall come upon thee, and shall pursue thee, and overtake thee, till thou be destroyed; because thou hearkenedst not unto the voice of the Lord thy God, to keep his commandments and his statutes which he commanded thee:"* These scriptures and many more show that God actually curses and it is carried out by His divine decree. In some cases, God curses and it becomes door opener for the enemy. 1 Samuel 16:14 *"But the Spirit of the Lord departed from Saul, and an evil spirit from the Lord troubled him."* And in fact the whole of that 16th chapter makes references to evil spirit coming from God to torment Saul! How can we comprehend that the Divine God has an evil spirit?

This is where some biblical school of thought says God works with the devil!

In Judges 9:23, *"Then God sent an evil spirit between Abimelech and the men of Shechem; and the men of Shechem dealt treacherously with Abimelech:"*

Some Christians argue that in the New Testament, Christ has redeemed us from the curse by taking our place whilst others are of the view that God does not curse anymore in this era of grace dispensation. Jesus said He came to do what He saw His Father do and He has come to do the will of that Who sent Him! But we saw Him cursing a fig tree, which withered to the roots in Matthew 21:18-22. In Matthew 11:20-25, Jesus cursed three major cities where He did great and mighty works: Bethsaida, Chorazin and Capernaum.

Will it logically follow that He saw His Father pronouncing curses? In fact, the tree dying or withering to the roots gives the revelation of how a curse works. We shall discuss that in subsequent chapters.

Having my own way, I will say the devil has no power to curse! Of course he is roaring like a lion seeking whom he can devour! He is looking for open doors. That is why he is the accuser of the brethren. He accuses to get access to carry out curses. He looks for ways to perpetuate or carry out what God has decreed against disobedient children. He also seeks to prevent the blessings God has ordained for His children. He sometimes sees the stars and destinies and fights them by going into the archives of families. That is the reason why we need not to be sinning, as this becomes the door opener for him. We should be aware that Satan is not omniscient or omnipotent as our God is! He cannot be everywhere at the same time! Remember he said he has been going up and down? Rather, he has a very well structured systems and agents who are deployed everywhere to send information. He has a very good network that is highly effective. There are other sources of curse from people representing Satan such as witch doctors etc. Unscriptural or evil covenants as seen in the freemason or occultism are all open doors through which Satan carries out curses.

'Soulish' prayers or utterances are other sources of placing curses. The soul has a lot of power over both good and evil. This evil part of the soul is what many bible scholars call Christian witchcraft. When you (as a Christian or born again believer) pray evil from your soul instead of Holy Ghost inspired prayers or you make unholy utterances on someone. This is a very dangerous channel that the devil uses against Christians but we blindly turn it to mean God answered prayers! Proverb 6:2 *"Thou art ensnared by the words of thy mouth."* Some so called men of God pray such prayers for members who had left or members who they see as 'problematic members'; spouses pray such prayers especially for unsaved spouses, parents pray such prayers for children and Christians pray it against each other.

Man (as a creation) can also pronounce curses. We are familiar with this and a lot of biblical examples proof this as well. Parents or persons with relational authority such as fathers and husbands can pronounce curse as in the cases of Noah, Isaac and Jacob. An example in the bible is when Laban's daughter Rebekah stole his household gods and Laban accused Jacob of doing it. Upset that Laban was accusing him of the act, Jacob said, in Genesis 31:32 *"With whomsoever thou findest thy gods, let him not live: before our brethren discern thou what is thine with me, and take it to thee. For Jacob knew not that Rachel had stolen them."* Here Jacob unknowingly pronounced death curse on his wife Rebekah and sure enough she died in childbirth when she was having her next child.

God's servants can also place curses. In Joshua 6:26 we read of Joshua (a servant of God) pronouncing these words: *"And Joshua adjured them at that time, saying, Cursed be the man before the Lord, that riseth up and buildeth this city Jericho: he shall lay the foundation thereof in his firstborn, and in his youngest son shall he set up the gates of it."*

Moses in Deuteronomy 27, pronounced many curses on Mount Ebal and in Numbers 16: 28 he cursed Korah and his followers; David also in 2 Sam 1:21 pronounced these curses: *"Ye mountains of Gilboa, let there be no dew, neither let there be rain, upon you, nor fields of offerings: for there the shield of the mighty is vilely cast away, the shield of Saul, as though he had not been anointed with oil."* 2 Sam 1: 16 *And David said unto him; "Thy blood be upon thy head; for thy mouth hath testified against thee, saying, I have slain the Lord's anointed."* Reading from 1 Kings 17, Elijah, (a Prophet of God) cursed the city with drought and Elisha also placed a curse on some children in 2 Kings 2:23-25 and in 2 Kings 5, we see Elisha again cursing his servant Gehazi.

Sometimes, so called interventionism or support for children (special children) inflict demons on these children so that the 'specialists' would have their data and get works to do. They nail children, pin them, tag them and they may never come out.

We can curse ourselves! We can impose curses on ourselves with the utterances we make. There are a number of persons in the bible who put curses on themselves. In Genesis 27:13, Rebekah caused a curse upon herself when Jacob asked her if his father found out he wasn't Esau if he Jacob would not get a curse instead of a blessing. She replied and said; *"...Upon me be thy curse, my son: only obey my voice, and go fetch me them."* Also in Matthew 27:24 & 25 when Pilate washed his hand renouncing any guilt of Jesus' death and the people said *"His blood be on us and on our children."*

As I said in the earlier chapter, minor, momentary advantage or a seemingly inconsequential act, behavior, decision or standard can have important and irreversible influences on the lives of majority of people and situations for a long period of time. The easiest or common way to bring about these influences is sin- the sin of rebellion and disobedience. I however emphasize that there are many ways of bringing in a curse but involvement in sins is the easiest way to bring curses upon our lives and children. I have observed and studied six major ways that serve as root causes for curses.

First and foremost is the shedding of innocent blood. *"And the LORD said unto Cain, Where is Abel thy brother? And he said I know not: Am I my brother's keeper? And he said, what hast thou done? The voice of thy brother's blood crieth unto me from the ground. And now art thou cursed from the earth, which hath opened her mouth to receive thy brother's blood from thy hand."* Genesis 4:9-11.

Cain murdered his brother Abel because of jealousy. God refused Cain's offering but received the firstlings from Abel. By murdering his brother, he opened himself up for a curse. In Genesis 49:5-7, Jacob cursed his sons Simeon and Levi for shedding blood. *"Then there was a famine in the days of David three years, year after year; and David enquired of the Lord. And the Lord answered, It is for Saul, and for his bloody house, because he slew the Gibeonites"* 2 Samuel 21:1.
These and many other biblical scriptures underline the fact that shedding blood is a root cause for curses.
Simeon and Levi, sons of Jacob were cursed because they shedded blood. (Genesis 49:5-7)

Secondly, sexual perversion can also trigger a curse. For example, Canaan, a grandson of Noah, was cursed for sexual perversion. *"And Noah began to be an husbandman, and he planted a vineyard: And he drank of the wine, and was drunken, and he was uncovered within his tent. And Ham, the father of Canaan, saw the nakedness of his father and told his two brethren without. And Shem and Japheth took a garment, and laid it upon both their shoulders, and went backward, and covered the nakedness of their father and their faces were backward, and they saw not their father's nakedness. And Noah awoke from his wine and knew what his younger son had done unto him. And he said Cursed be Canaan; a servant of servants shall he be unto his brethren"* Genesis 9:20-25. Canaan, a grandson of Noah, was cursed because of what bible scholars and some theologians argue to be sexual perversion because his father Ham saw the nakedness of his father.

Noah spoke a curse over his grandson Canaan, son of Ham. It is clear that the iniquity of Ham was transferred down the family tree and affected his family lineage.

Noah's prophecy was fulfilled when the Canaanites became "hewers of wood and drawers of water for the Israelites" (Joshua 9:23). Jacob, also Israel, pronounced negative words on his first son Reuben because of sexual immorality in Genesis 49:3-4. We also see in Deuteronomy 23:2 *"A bastard shall not enter into the congregation of the Lord; even to his tenth generation shall he not enter into the congregation of the Lord."* Because of the parents' sin of fornication, a curse came upon generations. And if you follow the genealogy of this story, one will affirm that a lot happened and it took ten generations (which was David) to break this curse.

A third way curses are attracted is by bringing abominations; morally disgusting objects, or idols into one's house. *"The graven images of their gods shall ye burn with fire: thou shalt not desire the silver or gold that is on them, nor take it unto thee, lest thou be snared therein: for it is an abomination to the LORD thy God. Neither shalt thou bring an abomination into thine house, lest thou be a cursed thing like it: but thou shalt utterly detest it, and thou shalt utterly abhor it; for it is a cursed thing"* Deuteronomy 7:25-26. We should not forget Rachel who stole his father's god, hid it and then received a cursed from her husband (Genesis 31:19). These items include such perverse things as demonic objects, some types of jewellery, paintings, art, books, music, games, videos, and occult items.

Rebuilding what God destroyed is also another way of bringing curses. *"And Joshua adjured them at that time, saying, Cursed be the man before the LORD, that riseth up and buildeth this city Jericho: he shall lay the foundation thereof in his firstborn, and in his youngest son shall he set up the gates of it"* Joshua 6:26.
When a person repents or is saved by grace, he or she receives forgiveness and freedom from the powers of darkness. If a person rebuilds or reintroduces into the life of this saved soul anything the Holy Spirit once destroyed, that person receives a curse for doing that. (Matthew12:43-45). For example, ungodly soul ties and family curses that were broken by the power of the Spirit, addictions and sexual perversions, or spiritualism and witchcraft. To introduce bondage anew into a person's life brings a curse. Again, anyone that introduces or entices a person to sin also receives a curse. That was why the serpent, Eve and Adam were all cursed in Genesis 3.

Fifthly, when one operates in a Jezebel spirit, it brings a curse. (Even though, the Bible does not mention a Jezebel spirit, but in 1 and 2 Kings, stories of Jezebel has been told in detail. This spirit is one of the most intelligent demonic agents of Satan's kingdom. Its operations constitutes sexual immorality and controlling of people or organisations. Is an illegitimate authority that leads to rebellion and domination. If it possesses you, you could do the unthinkable. *And when Jehu came to Jezreel, Jezebel heard of it; she painted her face, and tied her head, and looked out at a window. And as Jehu entered in at the gate, she said, Had Zimri peace, who slew his master? And he lifted up his face to the window, and said, 'Who is on my side?' Who? And there looked out to him two or three eunuchs. And he said, 'Throw her down.' So they threw her down, and some of her blood was sprinkled on the wall, and on the horses: and he trod her under foot. And when he was come in, he did eat and drink, and said, 'Go, see now this cursed woman, and bury her: for she is a king's daughter'* 2 Kings 9:30-34. These wicked spirits in the world has chained thousands of people today. This is a controlling, manipulating, seducing and power hungry spirit. Following this spirit can get you killed. In the verses 35-36 of 2 Kings 9, Elijah pronounced a curse on Jezebel and her end.

And finally, the arrogance and pride also serve as channels for curses. *"Thou hast rebuked the proud that are cursed, which do err from thy commandments"* Psalms 119:21. Not everyone that starts out with Christ ends the race with Christ. Some err and lose their way. There are many arrogant secular humanists in this world for example that refuse to acknowledge the lordship of Christ. Some of these were once leaders of Christian churches, others not. Just like Pharaoh they say in their hearts, *"Who is the Lord that I should obey his voice?"* The arrogant and proud think more highly of themselves than they should. They feel themselves greater and above others. They are bumptious and puffed up.

Chapter 3
The Family Tree

When I ask *'there is a curse in this house, who brought it?'* I am drawing your attention to that peculiar thing in the house that has become common that everybody goes through or it affects everyone. I am talking about *The Family Tree! How does your family tree look like!* I mean the person up the family tree who was the cause of a curse that has become generational- the originator.

We have seen that curses don't come into a family without cause. It is a payment or "recompense for iniquity." It is written, in Lamentations 3:64-66, *"Render unto them a recompense, O LORD, according to the work of their hands. Give them sorrow of heart, thy curse unto them. Persecute and destroy them in anger from under the heavens of the LORD."*

By now I am sure with the help of the Holy Spirit you are reflecting back into your family tree. The first thing is to know what have been the recurring things that attack the family. Before one pinpoints (generational) curses, we need to identify what they look like. Let us be mindful however that having one of the enlisted in your life or family may not necessarily indicate a family curse, but to have several "recurring" ones might. It is also very important that one seeks the help of the Holy Spirit to help identify a curse. May He give you revelation as you read on.

One thing to note is that whenever a curse becomes generational the demon goes down from family to family. Each person of the family the demons stopped with, it gains more strength and grounds. It is worth knowing that a child can be inhabited by the family demon, which can remain dormant until awakened by sin!

From all that we have read, we know what curses are, their sources and how they come about. It would be necessary for us to identify a curse, know how it works and then take steps to deal with it. The book of Deuteronomy (28:1-64) spells out quite substantial and detail curses, I will make references to ten signs of these curses that have been common to man.

Emotional Instability, Fear As a Curse

"The LORD shall smite thee with madness, and blindness, and astonishment of heart" (**Deuteronomy 28:28**).

The first curse I will discuss is emotional instability. Take note- the Scripture above says the Lord will "smite with madness." To be smitten with madness means insanity, craziness, foolishness, irrational behaviour, depression, anger, rage and flakiness. The scripture also uses the term "blindness." This blindness releases confusion, indecision, and wonderment. If that's not enough the scripture follows that with "astonishment of heart" which means a trembling, unsettled, and fearful heart.

Under this curse, one is easily overcome by emotions and fear. This triggers a person to make foolish decisions and do crazy self-destructive things. A person in such condition has a continual inner struggle, internal warfare, and frustration. Two key signs of this family curse are confusion and depression. This curse explains why some people are double-minded and have problems ordering their lives with the Word of God and renewing their minds.

Hereditary Family Sicknesses

"The LORD shall make the pestilence cleave unto thee, until he has consumed thee from off the land, whither thou goest to possess it. The LORD shall smite thee with consumption, and with a fever, and with inflammation, and with an extreme burning, and with the sword, and with blasting, and with mildew; and they shall pursue thee until thou perish" (**Deuteronomy 28:21**). This curse releases sicknesses of all kinds.

In this case, the demon or spirit would write an extra code within the person's DNA and then would send a message to the body to put an additional function in the body that is not normal. Its reoccurrence then becomes an indication of a family curse. Let's take note of the terms "pestilence", "consumption", "fever" and "inflammation." These indicate a curse that is evidenced by arthritis. Inflammation of the brain and other organs lead to some strange diseases. Then we read the term "extreme burning" which points toward all sorts of strange fevers. I am not saying all fevers are curses.

Chronic Wounds

"The Lord will smite thee with the botch of Egypt, and with the emerods, and with the scab, and with the itch, whereof thou canst not be healed" (**Deuteronomy 28:27**). Those that have problems with wounds that will not heal experience these. Scripture also says, *"The LORD shall smite thee in the knees, and in the legs, with a sore botch that cannot be healed, from the sole of thy foot unto the top of thy head"* (**Deuteronomy 28:35**). This curse attacks legs, soles of the feet and the top of one's head. The Lord didn't leave any diseases out of this curse. He declared, *"Also every sickness, and every plague, which is not written in the book of this law, them will the LORD bring upon thee until thou be destroyed"* (**Deuteronomy 28:61**).

Barrenness, Impotence, Female Problems

"Cursed shall be the fruit of thy body, and the fruit of thy land, the increase of thy kine, and the flocks of thy sheep" **Deuteronomy 28:18**.

The word body, (in Hebrew is beten), which means womb, belly, or abdomen. The womb deals with reproduction. Signs of this curse are infections, hormone problems, menstrual problems, cramps, fibroids, painful sex, barrenness, miscarriages, cysts, tumours, bladder problems, and kidney stones. Some menstrual problems may be the result of a family curse. Men too can manifest this curse with erectile dysfunction and impotence.

Family Breakdowns, Divorce

This curse manifest in several ways including divorce, family divides, fights among relatives, families that scatter, no fellowship, jailed children, children born out of wedlock, and estranged relationships.

"Thou shalt betroth a wife, and another man shall lie with her: thou shalt build a house, and thou shalt not dwell therein: thou shalt plant a vineyard, and shalt not gather the grapes thereof" Deuteronomy 28:30.

Children are also affected by this family curse.
"Thy sons and thy daughters shall be given unto another people, and thine eyes shall look, and fail with longing for them all the day long: and there shall be no might in thine hand" Deuteronomy 28:32. This particular curse is becoming eminent as most parents are losing their children to evil pop culture; children becoming more obedient to teachers, social/welfare workers and friends instead of parents; some children being taken into social service care in some advanced countries; laws in

some countries give less rights to parents making them helpless leading to the loss of their children.

"Thou shalt beget sons and daughters, but thou shalt not enjoy them; for they shall go into captivity" Deuteronomy 28:41.

The iniquities of the fathers are visited on the children, which lead to many children being born in fatherless and single-parent homes, children becoming latchkey kids, kids on drugs, youth suicides, teen pregnancies and jailed juveniles.

Lack, Poverty, Inability To Produce

"Cursed shall be thy basket and thy store (kneading trough)" Deuteronomy 28:17.

"And thou shalt grope at noonday as the blind gropeth in darkness, and thou shalt not prosper in thy ways: and thou shalt be only oppressed and spoiled evermore, and no man shall save thee" Deuteronomy 28:29.

This is a curse on finances. A kneading trough is where food is prepared so I am likening this to the ability to produce. One is able to build wealth through production. Under this curse, one's ability to get wealth is stopped. People under this curse never have anything saved. Bill collectors continually oppress them and the spoilers steal what little they accumulate.

Debtors

These same people are slaves to their creditors. Poverty, lack and unexplained scarcity are very eminent with this curse. Scripture declares, *"Because thou served not the LORD thy God with joyfulness, and with gladness of heart, for the abundance of all things; Therefore shalt thou serve thine enemies that the LORD shall send against thee, in hunger, and in thirst, and in nakedness, and in want of all things: and he shall put a yoke of iron upon thy neck until he has destroyed thee"* Deuteronomy 28:47-48.

A person under this curse will squander, waste and get further in debt and bondage. They are candidates for get-rich schemes of all kinds. Those who do not squander money run into mysterious debts. Some work very hard but has nothing to show for.

No Ambition, Vision, Direction

"And thou shalt grope at noonday as the blind gropeth in darkness, and thou shalt not prosper in thy ways: and thou shalt be only oppressed and spoiled evermore, and no man shall save thee" Deuteronomy 28:29.

I have met those that have no internal vision for their lives. They set no goals and are blown to and fro by lives circumstances. This curse is revealed in those without ambition. They go aimlessly through life. They lack the strong desire to make a difference in life, vision, dream, or aspiration to succeed. Those under this curse care less about tomorrow. They are without hope and terribly negative. They "grope" as "blind men" with no direction, always uncertain and full of apathy and full of Luke warmness.

Bondage And Slavery

"The stranger that is within thee shall get up above thee very high, and thou shalt come down very low. He shall lend to thee, and thou shalt not lend to him: he shall be the head, and thou shalt be the tail" Deuteronomy 28:43-44.

This person loses his individualism, liberty, and freedom. They are easily controlled and manipulated into a loss of identity. They lose their freedoms, can't make decisions on their own, and must get permission from their masters. Under this curse, most people end up looking to other gods for provision and protection, not unto the Lord. They become faithless, carnal, and full of idolatry, entertainment, and anything that divides them from the lordship of Christ.

Addiction, premature death

This includes but not limited to drugs, alcohol, sex and pornography. In some families, members are prone to accidents and premature death.

Almost There Syndrome

Some people experience this most of their lives and their children and grandchildren in different ways. With some people, as they get close to receiving good news or achieving something great, something sets in or pops up to prevent them from celebrating. This includes but not limited to promise and fail, disappointment and non-achievement or non-fulfillments.

Curses Without A Cause

We have understood that curses don't visit a family without cause. However, there are curses without causes! It is without cause because the victims were not the actual originators or actors that warranted the punishment or curse. The Israelites believed that they were being punished for sins they did not commit. Lamentations 5:7, *"Our **fathers** have sinned, and are not; and **we** have borne (been punished for) **their** iniquities."* However, we should not forget what God told them because naturally it sounds unfair for God to punish children for the sins of their fathers. For me there is more to it than that. The effects of sin are naturally passed down from one generation to the next. When a parent has a sinful lifestyle, the children are likely to practice the same sinful lifestyle. So if the children choose to repeat the sins of their parents, they will receive the judgement given their forefathers. That is why God said the soul that sins shall die. So, it is not unjust for God to punish sin to the third or fourth generation – those generations are committing the same sins their ancestors did. We will dig deeper in the next chapter when we talk about how curses are sponsored or get activated. Rachel in Genesis 35:17-18 cursed her son at birth. It took Jacob to reverse the curse else that innocent child would have been cursed for no reason. A similar case is found in 2 Kings 20; King Hezekiah acted wrongly and received a message from God through His Prophet. His response was that, *"will there not be peace and truth at least in my days?"* what this means is that the curse is waiting for his unborn descendants. When Noah left the ark, God blessed him and his sons. Thereafter, no one including Noah could curse what God had blessed as Balaam later discovered. How could it be that it was Ham who made fun of Noah and yet he (Noah) cursed his grandson Canaan? I think it was because he couldn't curse Ham. Noah knew this principle and since he couldn't curse Ham, he cursed his grandson Canaan. He was the innocent recipient of a curse meant for his father. Shimei son of Gera, cursed David as he saw him approaching. David did nothing to call for that curses.

I must draw readers attention to this revelation: that curses in any kind as outlined above may not always show up or take the same root. I have said in the earlier chapters that curses can be of a particular pattern. Yes, but the enemy is cunning.

Once I overheard from the kitchen as my little son watched cartoon in the living room. I could hear one 'evil character' fighting someone and making references. The victim said *"I thought you were dead ages! You were killed ancient times! Then the evil character busted into an evil laughter and said 'do I die! Did I hear you say I was killed ancient times! Never! I don't die! I only go into hibernation! I only wait quietly for a moment such as this and then bounce back! I bounce back not as before so you may think I am no more but I have always been around and always around looking for new ways to re-introduce myself and re-live my life!"* I was scared but quickly caught a very deep revelation. I bet the producer or writer may not be a Christian but any other spiritualist who understood how spirits operate. I quickly asked my son to quit watching whilst I pondered over that information.

Then I remembered a book I read years back that talked about how curses come back alive. There is no duration or time span for curses to end! You cannot deal enough with curses. I recall how the author revealed how curses make their ways back into people's life generationally. According to the author, she was a shopaholic! She could not do a single day without shopping. She did not use most things she bought but only took delight in spending. Until a deliverance minister delivered her and there was a revelation that she had inherited that curse from the father who was a severe alcoholic, she never knew the cause. Her grandfather was a womaniser who had to spend his money on prostitutes, his son (her dad) became alcoholic spending his money on hard liquors and the grand daughter (the author) spent her money on clothes and other stuff. It was the same curse manifesting in different forms! It was addiction! The lady may have said 'thank God I don't drink alcohol or married to alcoholic or spend my money on men so I have no problem but see how addiction manifested itself! It is true spirits don't die but go into hibernation and wait to resurface.

This is the reason why it is difficult to deal with curses. It is a subject Christians do not have to joke with! Some people do not even believe that a Christian can be cursed or carry a curse around whilst others do not even believe the vehicle (demons) deployed to carry it out. All you have to do is believe in Christ and nothing else can happen or harm you. And some even say the curses that God pronounced in the Old Testament were for some 'special or specific' people (Israelites and God's enemies). I always ask: if you believe the curses to be for some people, why don't you deny the blessings as well because the blessings were also for the Israelites and God's people! Both you and I were not there in any of these times yet we claim the blessings and still hold unto the word that He spoke unto them (and the word works and manifests in our lives today). We believe we are spiritual gentiles having been circumcised by faith and therefore we qualify for grace. So why then can't we accept the reverse and deal with the root causes as God gives us revelation? If we believe blessings to be real, so should we believe the curses and deal with them.

Chapter 4

Agents, Carriers, or Vehicles

So how does curse go into activation? What triggers a curse into motion? The number one factor that sponsors a curse is sin. The first curse that was pronounced by God was for Adam and Eve and it was pronounced when they had sinned in the garden. What was their sin? Simply put, sin of disobedience or rebellious. Sin is the easiest way to activate a curse. Because it moves you away from God into the open settings and this gives agents, vehicles the mandate to carry out curses. These agents or vehicles are called demons! I would want to show two clusters of texts that are both true, both inspired by God, both infallible and show how they fit together.

In **Exodus 20:5-6**, God says: *"Thou shalt not bow down thyself to them, nor serve them: for I the Lord thy God am a jealous God, visiting the iniquity of the fathers upon the children unto the third and fourth generation of them that hate me; And shewing mercy unto thousands of them that love me, and keep my commandments."*

And in **Exodus 34:6-7**, *"And the Lord passed by before him, and proclaimed, The Lord, The Lord God, merciful and gracious, longsuffering, and abundant in goodness and truth, Keeping mercy for thousands, forgiving iniquity and transgression and sin, and that will by no means clear the guilty; visiting the iniquity of the fathers upon the children, and upon the children's children, unto the third and to the fourth generation."*

Leviticus 26:39, *"And they that are left of you shall pine away in their iniquity in your enemies' lands; and also in the iniquities of their fathers shall they pine away with them."*

Deuteronomy 24:16, makes it clear that the *"Fathers shall not be put to death because of their children, nor shall children be put to death because of their fathers. Each one shall be put to death for his own sin."*

In **2 Kings 14:6**, *"But the children of the murderers he slew not: according unto that which is written in the book of the law of Moses, wherein the Lord commanded, saying, The fathers shall not be put to death for the children, nor the children be put to death for the fathers; but every man shall be put to death for his own sin."*

Finally **Ezekiel 18:20**, *"The soul that sinneth, it shall die. The son shall not bear the iniquity of the father, neither shall the father bear the iniquity of the son: the righteousness of the righteous shall be upon him, and the wickedness of the wicked shall be upon him."*

From the first part, we see that the sins of the fathers are punished in the children through those sins becoming the children's own sin. That is really crucial. In other words, the hatred of God is the embodiment of what the father's problem was. What we are told is that when father's sins are visited on the children it is because the children have become sinners like the fathers. The father's sins *are the children's sins.* So no innocent child has ever been punished for a father's sins; only guilty children are punished and are guilty of the **very sins** that their fathers sinned. That is our first observation.

Our second observation is, because of God's grace which is, of course, finally secured for us by Jesus on the cross, the children can confess their own sins and the sins of their fathers and be forgiven and accepted by God. Nobody is trapped in his father's sins — or even in his *own* sins. We already see it in **Leviticus 26:40-42** that,

"If they shall confess their iniquity, and the iniquity of their fathers, with their trespass which they trespassed against me, and that also they have walked contrary unto me; And that I also have walked contrary unto them, and have brought them into the land of their enemies; if then their uncircumcised hearts be humbled, and they then accept of the punishment of their iniquity: Then will I remember my covenant with Jacob, and also my covenant with Isaac, and also my covenant with Abraham will I remember; and I will remember the land."

So nobody in the Old Testament or the New Testament, under the New Covenant, is trapped or enslaved or in bondage or under an unbreakable curse because of something the fathers did, or something they did. God forgives the sins of those who repent.

Third observation makes us feel that none of these should make anyone feel trapped and without hope because the blood of Jesus conquers all sin and judgment for those who believe according to Acts 10:43.

From the above scriptures we can clearly see that sin is the only way or channel that can allow a curse to work in our lives. You may see yourself as a born again and so may not be repeating the sins of your parent(s). Let us use the first commandment of God in Exodus 20 alongside my personal story to explain the above scriptures and then we can draw conclusion.

In Exodus 20:3-4 God makes it clear that we should have no other gods before Him. We should not make for ourselves any image in the form of anything in heaven above or on the earth beneath or in the waters below. And we should not bow down to them or worship them; for He the Lord our God, is a jealous God.

It is understatement to say that God hates idolatry! Like I said my grandfather was guilty of this and therefore he sinned against God. Logically, from the first part of the scriptures, our first observation makes it clear that God will punish him for serving a graven image. How do I get punished too since I have not gone to bring any graven image nor serve one? How does his curse affect me? If anything at all, we have done our best to return it. Take your time to read the link and interpretation! I would be equally punished when I serve other gods apart from Yahweh. How? Clearly speaking and simply put, anything that takes your attention, anything you give priority and involve time and other resources on which gives satisfaction fully or partially, is a god! So anything that is amplified more or instead of Christ is a god! For example, as a pastor, if I choose to popularise myself instead of preaching Christ; I fail to preach the death and resurrection; the salvation message of the cross; I am equally guilty as my grandfather! Can you relate to this in your personal life?

In the second observation, grace has abound for us so if I renounce the sins and the acts of my grandfather and I live a life exclusive to Exodus 20:3-4, God will not punish me with my grandfather's sin.

The third observation makes it plain that no matter what happened in the past or what is happening now in the present, there is grace enough to right everything. The blood has paid for it.

The problem with us Christians of today is that we are like the Pharisee in Luke 18:9 who went to the temple to pray and justified himself. He wasn't even aware of his sins and pride would not let him know. Such has been our lot today. When you talk about curses, people and for that matter (born again) Christians quickly jump to quote scriptures: *"therefore, if anyone is in Christ... curse is anyone that hangs on a tree..."* yet you look at this person and you see the same mishap and pattern that has been happening in their home. The mother married too late; deaths of first-born; divorce; childbirth without marriage, adultery etc. etc. it is a (particular) curse that comes with a particular sin against God! What do we mean at all? Why does Adam's sin still relate to us even after Christ's death? From a physical standpoint, the blood of Adam and Eve became corrupt and Leviticus 17:11 tells us *"…the life of the flesh is in the blood…"* The curse that Adam received for violating God's law (disobedience and rebellion) was transferred to his offspring – us. We are rebellious and disobedient. The curse that our ancestors received for their sins transfers to us because we are flesh, and the blood gives us life! But ignorantly, we misquote the bible and Satan deploys his agents who also execute a perfectly job through ignorance.

Should we take the rest of the commandments and examine our lives with them, we would be surprised at the revelation that the Holy Spirit would give us. If we would circumcise our hardened hearts and ask God to reveal to us what we need to know about curses in our family, we would be amazed at the things He will show us from generations until now.

Concluding this chapter, I will clear and emphatically say that curses are real and sin (of any kind) is the only way to keep doors opened for its activation. The continuation or perpetuation is through ignorance. There is a popular saying today in the world that "what you don't know cannot harm/kill you". I refuse that because it is what we don't know that is killing us!

Chapter 5
Dealing With Curses

In this concluding chapter, we would be talking about how we can deal with curse: how one can free themselves from any entanglement. By the end of this chapter, you can either learn how to 'rise up and walk' with the anointing and power God has given you so as to be able to do battles or you can choose to hide your head in the sand and let demons keep tearing you and your family to pieces. The apostle Paul could not have said it any better when he said that our real battle in this life is not with flesh and blood, but with principalities and powers. **(Ephesians 6:12 KJV)**

Yes spiritual warfare is real, sometimes the enemy can take things you read or hear and twist it around to scare you. He can even take scripture and twist it to scare you. So by the end of the book, the choice would be yours but I pray that you will have enlightenment.

Before we get into exactly the areas that the enemy uses as stand points, I want to give you some very basic verses from the Bible showing the importance that our Saviour Jesus Christ places on dealing with demons so that we realise the reality of demonic spirits in this world, and for us not to be afraid but engage and cast them out when we do run across them in life. I refer to demons throughout because they are the agents or vehicles that carry out curses. Dealing with them results in breaking or dealing with curses.

Here are 8 very powerful verses but not limited to from the Bible, all showing us that we are not to be afraid of demons, and that we are to directly engage with them if we have to, operating under God's authority and anointing to be able to do so.

1. *"And he said unto them, Go ye into all the world, and preach the gospel to every creature. He that believeth and is baptized shall be saved; but he that believeth not shall be damned.* And these signs shall follow them that believe; ***In my name shall they cast out devils;*** *they shall speak with new tongues;* They shall take up serpents; and if they drink any deadly thing, it shall not hurt them; they shall lay hands on the sick, and they shall recover." **(Mark 16:15-18)**

2. *"And Jesus returned in the power of the Spirit into Galilee: and there went out a fame of him through all the region round about. And he taught in their synagogues, being glorified of all. And he came to Nazareth, where he had been brought up: and, as his custom was, he went into the synagogue on the sabbath day, and stood up for to read. And there was delivered unto him the book of the prophet Esaias.*

And when he had opened the book, he found the place where it was written, The Spirit of the Lord is upon me, because he hath anointed me to preach the gospel to the poor; he hath sent me to heal the brokenhearted, **to preach deliverance to the captives,** *and recovering of sight to the blind,* **to set at liberty them that are bruised,**" **(Luke 4:14-18)**

3. "*Behold, I give unto you* **power to tread on serpents and scorpions,** *and over all the power of the enemy: and nothing shall by any means hurt you.*" **(Luke 10:19)**

4. "*Then he called his twelve disciples together,* **and gave them power and authority over all devils,** *and to cure diseases.*" **(Luke 9:1)**

5. "*And he called unto him the twelve, and began to send them forth by two and two;* **and gave them power over unclean spirits;...** *And they cast out many devils, and anointed with oil many that were sick, and healed them.*" **(Mark 6:7, 13)**

6. "*And when he had called unto him his twelve disciples, he* **gave them power against unclean spirits,** *to cast them out, and to heal all manner of sickness and all manner of disease.*" **(Matthew 10:1)**

7. "*But go rather to the lost sheep of the house of Israel. And as ye go, preach, saying, The kingdom of heaven*

*is at hand. Heal the sick, cleanse the lepers, raise the dead, **cast out devils: freely ye have received, freely give.** " (Matthew 10:6-8)*

8. *"He that committeth sin is of the devil; for the devil sinneth from the beginning. For this purpose the Son of God was manifested, **that he might destroy the works of the devil.** " (1 John 3:8)*

If you will notice from the above, every time Jesus gave His apostles the power and command to go out and walk with His anointing, He always told them to cast out demons/devils as one of His specific commands – no exceptions!

So if Jesus was constantly casting out demons, always telling the apostles to cast out demons, and the apostles too were always casting out demons, then it should only be logical that the Church should continue to still cast out demons when needed.

It has been estimated by many Bible scholars that approximately 25% of the miracles Jesus had performed were Him casting demons out of people. Satan and his demons are not confined to the bottomless pit yet. And this will not happen until Jesus returns back to us in His second coming. Until that event happens, Satan and his demons are still free to roam in the "air" seeking who they are going to try and devour next. So what will be their work if not to fight, frustrate, torment and distract us?

As Christians, we always have to remember that the devil and his demons are already defeated foes. Jesus has already defeated Satan at the cross when He was crucified.

What is now left is that all Christians have to realise that the victory is already ours. We have the antidote for the enemy.
We thus have to learn how to engage and defeat the devil and his demons when they do try to move in. if we fail to do this, the enemy and his team will continue to use history or our background against us in the pretence of ignorance.

Depending on what you may be dealing with in your present set of circumstances and what you may have in your past background having knowledge can really help you in being able to plan and carry out the appropriate battle strategy.

First and foremost, the demons that carry out curses will try and attack you from an **outside position**, which means they are attacking you from the **"air."** These may be coming at you from the outside of your being. This means the attack is with no legal rights. For most Christians and people, this first level will be the one they will probably have to face the most from time to time.
Our Master Jesus Christ Himself had to face Satan head on with this kind of an outside attack when God led Him into the wilderness for 40 days and nights. In that wilderness setting, Satan was allowed to literally tempt Jesus with three specific temptations.
If God allowed His Son to be tempted in this manner, then you know the chances are very good that many of us

will have to face this same kind of demonic attack from time to time from this same kind of outside position.

The other is the **inside position**, which means they are attacking you from the inside of your body. And if this happens then it means something might have happened that has given them the legal right to be able to enter. Popular examples include Moses who had the spirit of anger from his bloodline.

Your job will then be to find out what their legal right is so that you can get it properly broken before God the Father. Once you have properly broken all of their legal rights before God the Father, then you can turn around and command them to now leave you in the name of Jesus.

But whether you are dealing with demons attacking you from an outside position or from an inside position – the rules are still the same.

Find out what their legal rights are, properly break those legal rights before God the Father, and then turn around and verbally cast all of them out in the name of our Lord and Saviour Jesus Christ.

Many believe that once you are saved and become born again, the old has past- behold all things are new so demons cannot enter in on the inside of you. The Bible tells us that the Holy Spirit will literally come in and enter in on the inside of your human spirit at the moment of your conversion with Jesus. As a result, our bodies now become the temple of the Holy Spirit, they believe there is no way that a demon or a group of demons can enter in on the inside of your body.

At first glance, this does appear to be a very logical argument. However, what they are missing is the fact that the Bible tells us that we have three, distinct, separate parts to our being. We have a body, a soul, and a spirit. The Holy Spirit is living and dwelling in your human spirit, but He is not living up in your soul or body area.

If a Christian ends up committing a severe, door-opening sin and transgression against the Lord, this gives the demons full legal right to be able to directly attack. Then what the demons will try and do is to try and enter that person's body and soul. They will not be able to enter into the Christian's spirit because the Holy Spirit is already living in there. But they will be able to enter into the body and soul of that person.

I would advise readers to talk to any deliverance minister who does deliverances on a regular basis. They will all tell you that demons can enter in on the inside of a Christian, and that they then have to be cast out of them by way of an actual deliverance. In fact, they cannot cast the demons out of a person unless that person is a Christian to begin with, or unless that person is willing to become a Christian if they are not saved.

If an unsaved person has demons living and operating on the inside of them, they will have no spiritual authority to be able to cast the demons out of them. This kind of deliverance is only available for born-again Christians.

This debate has been going on for a long time in the Body of Christ and will obviously never be resolved anytime in the near future. The only thing that I can personally tell you is that I have come across quite a few Christians who have had demons literally dwelling on the inside of them and they all had to have the demons cast out of them by way of an actual deliverance.

I know for sure there are big debates going on right now in the Body of Christ about how far demons can go with Christians. There are lists of best books ever written on the subject of deliverance and engaging with demons. Each one of these books have been written by very credible, anointed men and women of God who have learned much in this area of spiritual warfare and with lots of life and ministry experiences. And what you will outstandingly find out from each of them is that they all underline real battlefields of life where this kind of activities do exist, and show that Christians can draw demons on the inside of them if they have the appropriate legal rights to be able to enter!

One thing I know for sure is our God (the Father) is a "Man of War," and He has a war side to His personality. He does not hesitate to go into battle for us if we are willing to stand up and fight your enemies as a true soldier of Jesus Christ.

But before God can go into battle for His child, one will first have to be willing to march on to that battlefield and face the enemy head on like David did with Goliath.

Jesus Christ our Saviour has already given us His power, His anointing, and His authority to cast out demons and to trample over all the power of our enemies.

It is simply a matter of each and every Christian being willing to take up his sword, which is the Word of God, and verbally commanding the demons to leave you in the name of Jesus Christ. It is really that simple in this first level of spiritual warfare in dealing directly with any kind of demonic attack.

However, in the second level, things get much heavier because there is a full legal right.

This is the realm that gets many Christians in trouble with demons. What happens here is that someone has given some kind of legal right for the demons to be able to launch a full-scale operation.

We can confirm from the story of Job in the Bible (from the verse below) that we apparently have some kind of protective hedge around us that protects us from demonic spirits. *"Hast not thou made an HEDGE about him, and about his house, and about all that he hath on every side? thou hast blessed the work of his hands, and his substance is increased in the land."* **(Job 1:10)**

As a result of this protective hedge, there appears to be some kind of spiritual law in operation that demons have to abide by. They may occasionally be able to come against you as described in the first one, but they can easily be cast off from you by just issuing a good, basic, battle command.

However, what demons do is just wait for a believer to cause a hole to occur in their protective hedge. And how does this occur? By engaging and crossing over into any direct sins and transgressions that are expressly forbidden by God the Father in His Word!

Obviously not every sin and transgression will cause a hole to occur in your protective hedge with the Lord. The Bible tells us that we are all sinners and that we have all fallen short of the glory of our God. This is why Jesus had to come down to die on the cross – to pay the penalty for all of those sins, and to be able to give us full forgiveness and a full pardon for all of our sins.

If demons had a legal right to be coming after us every single time we sinned or transgressed, then none of us would ever be safe from their attacks, and we would all be in a state of constant warfare with them.

However, what many deliverance ministers have found out in the actual battlefields when having to deal direct with real live demons – is that there are certain sins and transgressions that will give demons the legal right to be able to launch a full scale attack against a person, even if that person is already a Christian!

Once you become saved and born again through the blood that Jesus Christ shed for us on the cross, this does not give you the right or the license to be able to keep on sinning.

Though we have all been made perfectly righteous in the eyes of God as a result of Jesus' righteousness now being imputed to us, we still have to make every effort on our end to stay on the righteous side of the fence in our walk with our Lord.

We have to do the best we can to try and live righteous lives and stay out of any sins and transgressions against our Lord – especially those of the heavier kind that will be listed below.

In this area there are certain types of sins and transgressions that will give demons the legal right to be able to come directly after you if God should so choose to allow this to happen. If you choose to engage in some of these (heavier) sins, then you could possibly break the protective hedge that you have around you with the Lord.

The demons will then be quick to see that opening when it does occur, and they will waste no time in trying to come directly after you.

Demons just wait for people, especially Christians, to cross over into any kind of door-opening, hedge-breaking sin and transgression, which will then give them the full legal right to be able to launch an all-out, full scale attack on that person and their life.

Here are some of the heavier sins and transgressions, which when committed with any type of frequency or intensity that can get one into major trouble.

As Christians, we can have absolutely no part in any of the following areas:

The occult
False religions or cults
Any part of the New Age Movement
Any type of Satan worshiping group
Any involvement with abortion or the abortion industry

Abusing alcohol
Doing any type of drugs – including pot
**Any type of extreme verbal and/or physical abuse
on your mate or children**
Any type of promiscuous, sexual lifestyle
Any type of criminal activity
Murder
Bringing a cursed object into your home

The last one point is what has been my lot and what has actually propelled me to write this book. I made it clear from the beginning how this cursed object has actually opened doors for the enemy to get my family and me. If you noticed, all of the above listed are things that one does out of own free will and volition against the Lord. These are all sins that you do and commit against the Lord out of one's own preference. In other words, these are all direct willful sins done against the Lord.

Each one of these areas is a major door opener to the dark side. All of these sins and behaviours are totally unacceptable in the eyes of God.

If you have drawn demons into your life as a result of engaging in one or more of the above door-opening sins, then what you will have to do before you can cast the demons out of your life is that you will have to fully break all of their legal rights. Once you have fully broken all of the legal rights that the demons have been feeding and operating on, then you will be able to turn around and verbally command them to now leave you in the name of Jesus Christ.

You will first have to realise that you have been sinning and transgressing directly against God by delving into any of the above areas.

Once you have full realisation and understanding that these are all unacceptable sins and behaviours before God, then you will have to go before God, fully confess out each one of the transgressions as actual sins, and then fully renounce each one of them – telling God that you will never, ever go back to any of them ever again.

Then once each of these sin areas have been fully confessed and fully renounced before the Lord – then you can turn around, take the authority that God has given you to trample over all the power of your enemy, and cast the demons off you for good.

What happens to some Christians, once they realise they have drawn demons into their lives as a result of being involved in some of the above sin areas – is that they will first try and cast the demons out before breaking their legal rights with God the Father. If you try and do this before you properly break their legal rights before God the Father, they will not go! I bet you!

The reason for this is that they know they still have the full legal right to stay attached to you since their legal rights have not been properly confessed out, renounced, and broken before God the Father.

To anyone who may have drawn heavy demonic activity in his or her life as a result of engaging in some of these heavier sins – remember – the only sin that cannot be forgiven is a direct blasphemy against the Holy Spirit. All other sins and transgressions can be forgiven, no matter how bad, how vile, and how severe you think they may be.

If you are truly sorry for having engaged in this kind of activity, fully willing to confess and renounce all of this activity before God the Father – then God can fully forgive you and fully deliver you from these demons and restore order back into your life. There is no hopeless situation before the Lord.

The third way a curse can work is by demons attacking as a result of what someone else may have done to you.

What happens in this area is that sometimes demons come in and attach themselves to a person as a result of what someone else may have done to that person. This may include the examples of women who have been raped, people who have been ritually abused in (satanic) groups, people who have been victims of certain types of crimes and assault, women who may have been severely physically abused by their husbands or partners, and children who have been severely abused by one or both parents – either physically or verbally.

What happens in some of these types of extreme cases is that demons, once they see that person being physically violated to this kind of an extreme degree, will realize that there might be a hole in that person's hedge. What demons look out for is the person or victim's response to the violation. For example, if a woman has been raped, the demons will see if that person will start to exhibit and manifest emotions of hatred, anger, bitterness, and unforgiveness.

Once they see this kind of an opening, they will then try and move in to see if they can attach themselves to that person.

But if that person does not start to work out these kinds of negative emotions over a certain period of reasonable time, then the demons will have something they can attach themselves to, and that something are the negative emotions of hatred, bitterness, and extreme anger that will settle in that person's mind, spirit, and emotions over a certain period of time.

Chapter 6

Life Journey Lesson as Shared by a Brother in the Lord

A True Story:

In the wisdom literature, Proverbs 26:2 King Solomon establishes a principle with respect to curses: *"As the bird by wandering, as the swallow by flying, so the curse causeless shall not come."*

I believe behind every curse that comes upon us there is a cause, hence the title of this book. This chapter is a true story, which for the purpose of anonymity the real identity of the main characters are somehow concealed. It talks about one of my nephews who volunteered to share his own life story as his contribution to this book. His own elder brother used witchcraft manipulations to destroy his life. This information lay bare the causes of curse that commonly afflict our lives. After reading this, you will be enlightened and apply God's solution. Let's read his story:

"I am younger to my brother (Frank Frimpong) born of the same parents into one of the Agona houses in Asamankese in the Eastern Region of Ghana. Our ancestry/genealogy connects to Opanin Kwadwo Okona, the man mentioned earlier on in this book as contracting idols into the family. Kwadwo Okona was very rich and he built several houses and various farms so that he was able to house and helped his five sisters and a brother and their generation. Unfortunately, in his bid to protect his riches and people he went for (idols) gods called Tigare. I quite remember when I was young I used to help carry some of the gods to the shrine where goats, sheep and dogs were sacrificed.

When I got to middle school I started attending Methodist Church because the school required it. With time I was baptized and joined the church choir because I was attracted to the songs. In all these, I didn't know the Lord Jesus Christ personally.

When it came to education it was very challenging: my father died when I was seven years old and my mom could not pay for my school fees. Fortunately my father's sister opted to take us through primary and middle school.

In form one my teachers paid for me to try the common entrance examinations and I passed with high marks but I couldn't go to secondary school because I didn't get anybody to help me. In form two my mother discouraged me from taking the examination again because there was no helper but the teachers registered me again and this time I topped the whole of Eastern region. As a result, a lot of schools offered me admission but because there was no helper I couldn't go. Finally my form one teacher Mr. Kwasi Adjei Twum took me to Asamankese secondary school and paid for me to start as day student. Subsequently, I won bursaries and scholarships and I went to the boarding house and that took me through secondary school, sixth form and university.

At the University I left the Methodist Church and joined an independent Baptist Church in Dansoman that preached "once saved forever saved". In all these I was not committed to the course of righteousness and holiness.

When I completed university of Ghana, I got a job immediately at Unilever Ghana limited (formerly U. A.C. Ghana Limited) trading division and after six months probation period I was confirmed as the Cash and Banking Manager supervising the cash and banking activities of one hundred and fifty depots throughout Ghana.

After two years I was transferred to Lever Brothers at Tema as Technical Statistics Manager accounting for production and works in progress and explaining variances. I also worked at other well-known companies such as S.C.O.A. Motors and Ashanti Goldfields Company. I held various good positions in good companies and things were going well for me. At a point my salary was US Dollar based. I tried to help all my siblings and extended family members and that was when I saw trouble.

I stopped going to church when things were going well for me because I got too busy chasing money and worldliness. I forgot completely that there's Tigare in my house. My own elder brother was used to bring me down and nearly killed me. It used to be the trend that our family members died at a very old age but when the gods began to strike people started dying at very young age. This is perceived to be the effect of the nominal worship of Tigare.

Finally our new and bold Abusuapanin returned the gods but it was too late. The gods have spread witchcrafts and sorcerers like wildfire in the family. Adult men and women and children have become agents of these gods spreading death, shame, disgrace and total destruction. God told the people of Israel in Deuteronomy 22:15 *that cursed be the man that maketh any graven or molten image, an abomination unto the Lord, the work of the hands of the craftsman, and putteth it in a secret place.* From this scripture it can be deduced that a curse was placed on the Agona family. Such curses are trans-generational following generation after generation. The only way to be free from these curses is to run to the Son of God and Saviour of this world (the Lord Jesus Christ) who can set you free indeed. He turns curses into blessings (Deut. 23:5).

The gods used my brother as a vessel to destroy me. He liked juju from infancy because he thought that would make him rich and powerful quickly. Resultantly, he became an easy tool for the gods. As I said I was helping all my siblings. This elder brother of mine was not working and had married with little children so I moved them to Accra and took very good care of them. I tried to help him travel outside to South Korea, China and Japan but in all three cases, he came back to Ghana after one to two weeks complaining that it was hard to live there. I also paid an agent to send him to the United States of America but he went to the agent to collect the money without my knowledge. I bought him a car and sent him to driving school and got him a driver's license so that he could drive his own taxicab to support himself and his household. Again, he went to defraud a pastor and the car was eventually seized and used to settle the case. Even that, our sister had to top up for his release.

Before I traveled to America I had twelve taxi cabs and eight "trotro" buses but Frank managed to sell all without giving anyone anything whatsoever.

As if that was not enough, my brother Frank accompanied by his friend went to a jujuman somewhere in the Volta region to do enchantments so that I would get a case at my work place that would bring me down. They eventually had a fight and these things were exposed. However I didn't take these warning signs serious and I went on with my life as usual and continued living in sin and trespasses.

Meanwhile my brother had graduated to Benin where he was getting his powers and I was thinking because I was helping people I didn't have to worry about anything not knowing that the curse on the Agona family still followed me.

I had a very big trouble of being charged with embezzlement of three hundred thousand dollars (US $300,000.00). My photo was published in the graphic newspaper. I was put in cells at the Police headquarters for eight and a half months before I was granted bail. At that time, Panin was telling people including family members that I would go to jail for more than thirty years and I don't know whether that was what his jujumen in Benin told him. When the judge gave me bail, Panin was so disappointed that he failed to show up to sign my bail papers. When I went to America, I studied for my masters in Accounting and General Administration. I also started a PhD program in leadership. I completed all the courses and was left with the dissertation. Three months into completing the program the embezzlement case arose with intensity.

When I got bail and I was out, my lawyer advised me to go on with my life while we dealt with the situation. Accordingly, I applied to some universities to teach and two of them gave me appointments as a lecturer in accounting to start in January 2011. I decided to spend the Christmas in my hometown Asamankese so that I can start teaching after that. On the 30th of December 2010 my sister asked me to drive her to Nsawam the next day to see somebody. So, I rose early 31st morning to have my bath to go and get my sister. While bathing I heard something hit my right shoulder. When I turned to check, I saw a short broom going up to hit again so I ran out of the bathroom and collapsed. I woke up three days later to find myself at the Saint Dominic's Hospital, Akwatia with a massive stroke. I was unable to talk with a thwarted face and the right side of my body from my head to my feet being paralysed. Fortunately, God was merciful to me and I didn't die. The doctors were able to stabilise me after a month. I was discharged and my sister took me to Akuapem Mampong to take care of me.

My wife and children abandoned me and they have stayed away from me till today and only they can explain that. At that time people became very scared of my brother because anyone who dared to confront him on an issue would be threatened with the gods to cause death, incapacitation or hardship. Thus, people feared to criticize him when he does the wrong thing. He therefore took advantage and took properties that didn't belong to him. He was already living in my house in Accra with his first wife and children and renting about eight bedrooms. He also took occupation of the family house at Asamankese with his second wife. In addition He exercised sole authority over a one-storey house containing eight bedrooms that belonged to my grandma and her children and was collecting the rents. Cocoa farms and other farms belonging to my grandma and her children were also taken over by him. He was just doing things with impunity because he realised people were afraid of him.

My mom, siblings, cousins, aunts, nieces, nephews and everybody were seriously afraid of him.

Initially my sister was taking care of me at Akuapem Mampong but Panin (Frank) managed to influence me to suspect my sister and my mother so I ran away to Accra.

I stayed in Accra for about two and a half years. During that period things became really rough and difficult. Later I learned that he clandestinely lured me to Accra to make sure that I would die. Things were so hard that getting money to buy food was difficult to get let alone what to buy medicine. But for the abundant mercies of God and the benevolence of some friends and relatives I would not have survived. After sometime I realized that if I had to get proper care, I had to go back to my sister and my mother at Akuapem Mampong. Accordingly I called my sister and after apologising profusely I told her of my situation and willingness to come back. My sister came for me and started taking care of me and I am very grateful. My health began to improve substantially and steadily. Then Panin (Frank) started attacking my mother and sister on their health because they were helping me to stay alive when he wanted me dead. He traveled to Benin frequently to make sure my mom and sister were dead.

At that time I didn't know what to do but God in his mercies sent missionaries to my house and they led me to Christ. They taught me about Christ and what to do to stay in the kingdom of God the Father and His son Jesus Christ. In spite of my situation they helped me to go to church every Sunday. I was subsequently baptized and received the Holy Spirit and I was added to the church.

I then decided to follow Jesus Christ by obeying Him so I can receive the blessings He has promised.

Not long after, my sister suffered a stroke and my eldest sister took her to a prayer camp near Larteh because they believed Panin was responsible. Unfortunately, after about two years they concluded that the pastor could not help them so they moved her to Kasoa, a place where they combined prayers and medicine.

Meanwhile at home the Holy Spirit was with us. My mother and the children in the house all got baptized and joined the church and we studied and prayed together.

I told my mother that the solution to my sister's problems is knowing Jesus Christ personally and obeying Him so she should go for my sister so she could give herself to Jesus Christ and seek medical help in addition but they thought the doctor at Kasoa could help her because he had helped other people. Eventually my sister died and things began to be difficult for me again. Meanwhile Panin and his wife and children were living in my house and renting eight bedrooms without giving me any money.

I told my pastor about my situation and he advised that we should fast and pray towards it. After we have fasted and prayed I told Panin that he has been living in my house for eighteen years so I want him to leave the house so I can have my house back but he refused to leave the house.

I found out that to file my case in court it would cost me 1,100 Ghc. Engaging the services of a lawyer would cost me at least 15,000 Ghc and I didn't have these kinds of money. I therefore sent him to the Rent Control department to see whether they could help me. When the Rent Control department invited him, he refused to go and wrote to them that he was not a tenant but a part owner of the house so they should advise me to take the case to court.

At that time he thought I could be affected by his juju so he intensified his actions to make sure I am dead or destroyed.

Meanwhile after about a year of his uncooperative attitude, the Rent Control department told me to pay 150 Ghc so that they could take the case to court on my behalf. I accordingly paid the money and the Rent Control department prepared a docket and sent the case to court.

Frank was very surprised when he got the summons from the court ordering him to appear before it in two weeks. He became very desperate because what he used to do before could not affect me anymore by the grace of God. He therefore travelled to Benin to consult his oracles. He came back assured that I would be dead before the court date. In fact, he told people how I would be dead soon. Three days before the court date he told my cousin at Amsterdam that something came to hit him hard while he was lying down. He told my cousin that because of what hit him, he was shaking violently and vigorously. Apparently he was thinking I have gone for juju that is stronger than what he had but I was obeying Jesus Christ and fasting and praying for God to protect and speak for me.

On the appointed date we met at court and the judge told him he should tell the court why he shouldn't give me back my house. He told the court that he has hired a lawyer but he couldn't come to court that day. The judge accordingly adjourned the case to two weeks. In two weeks he came to the court without the lawyer and the judge warned him that if he didn't file his defense by the next court date she would rule without his defense. The case was adjourned to another two weeks. In two weeks Panin became sick and couldn't come to court (they brought excuse duty from hospital) but his children filed the defense full of lies and without basis. Subsequently, the case was adjourned.

After the two weeks adjournment the children again brought excuse duty this time indicating that he was admitted at Ridge Hospital for kidney complications leading to a one-month adjournment. Unfortunately, he died after two weeks so on the scheduled court date, the wife and children couldn't come. I informed the judge of his death and the judge said that if that was the case the house falls back to me because the wife and children have no locum in the house. Accordingly, I had two options: to meet with the wife and children to give them some grace time to leave the house or hiring a lawyer to file a motion naming all of them and get court order to eject them.

I told the Abusuapanin about the situation and after deliberations we settled on giving them six months ending 31st March 2019 for the sake of Jesus Christ. I also found out that Panin has turned my house into living quarters and has converted kitchen and halls into bedrooms and had collected rent advances for two and three years ending 31st December 2020 but I still hope in the Lord to take care of me.

In conclusion, it is an established fact that the Agona family of Asamankese from Kwadwo Okona and his siblings and their generation were cursed according to the scriptures. Our dear children, siblings, cousins, aunties, uncles, nephews and nieces are involved in witchcrafts, sorceries and more idolatries. There are increasingly inexplicable deaths and destruction. People are being destroyed through drinking, smoking of cigarettes and marijuana, taking of cocaine and other such drugs. All these practices were initially foreign to the family. Nevertheless, the scriptures say in Deuteronomy 23:5 that God will turn all the curses into blessings when we run back to Him. If you are in a cursed family and you have not given your life to Jesus Christ as your Lord and Saviour, you are in danger so give your life to the Lord; accept Jesus as your personal savior and seek help immediately.

I close this chapter by personally testifying that God the Father and His son Jesus Christ lives and our prayers are answered when we depend on God. If we obey the commandments of the Lord and heed the promptings of the Holy Spirit to guide us, He will protect us from the wiles of the devil. He has done it for me by protecting me from all the attempts by my brother to kill me. I now live for the Lord and my health has improved tremendously. I know He has good plans to restore all that I have lost. He who started a good thing will bring it to a successful end in the name of Jesus Christ, Amen.

DECLARATION

1. I declare that henceforth, I refuse to be part of any law that was entered into at a witchdoctor's shrine that brings curses to the family in the name of Jesus.

2. Today in the name of Jesus, I declare war against the ancestral and demonic altars sponsoring attacks and curses to vex my life in Jesus name.

3. I declare that I am not part of what my ancestors promised, I refuse to be part of what I am not aware of and reject it in Jesus' name. And through the blood of the lamb, I set myself free even from those I knowingly or unknowingly got myself involved.

4. By the power of Jehovah God I access my God ordained blessings. I declare that henceforth I will swim in blessings in the name of Jesus.

5. Christ in me my hope of glory I subdue the power of anti-progress and stagnation in my bloodline. I declare that by divine acceleration I will excel in Jesus' name.

6. Today in the name of Jesus I take authority and come against evil family laws, demonic patterns and destroy them in Jesus' mighty name.

7. Spirit of the Living God fill me with eternal life and banish premature deaths from my family. I declare abundant life for me and my family in the name of Jesus.

8. I decree and declare that henceforth I disconnect myself from my bloodline and engraft to the family of Abraham in the mighty name of Jesus.

9. The Lord is holy, He is faithful He accomplishes what He starts. I receive total deliverance from demonic bondage and declare that I am free in the name of Jesus.

10. I decree and declare that my ministry is blessed, hallelujah! The Lord is moving me to a higher level. I am moving from grace to grace in the name of Jesus.

11. By the law of the resurrection of Jesus Christ of Nazareth, I decree and declare that my children will serve Jehovah God in the mighty name of Jesus Christ.

12. God, You are the God who recompense, I decree and declare that whatever was stolen from me, the Lord will give me double for my trouble and I will have substance for my bondage in Jesus' name.

13. The Lord is my shield, my protection and my stronghold. I declare when the enemy comes after me with his weapons, they will scatter in seven directions in the name of Jesus. Amen.

Prayer Points

(Self-cleansing and confession)

1. My Father, I thank you for the revelation knowledge through these teachings in the name of Jesus.

2. Father, I pray that You have mercy and forgive me of my sins and transgression that I committed against You. I ask for forgiveness in the mighty name of Jesus.

3. I repent and ask for forgiveness from any wrongdoing that opened door for the demonic altars to hold me in bondage in the mighty name of Jesus Christ of Nazareth.

4. Whatever I did knowingly or unknowingly blood of Jesus erase it and wash away my wrongdoings and close access for any legal rights for the devil to afflict me in the name of Jesus.

5. From today and now, I confess all my sins and the sins of my ancestors in the name of Jesus.

6. In the name of Jesus and His word in 1 John 1:9, I confess my sins for He is faithful and just to forgive me, therefore Lord, forgive me in the name of Jesus.

7. In the name of Jesus, I forgive those who trespassed against me. I totally forgive whoever that has offended me knowingly or unknowingly.

8. From today, the blood of Jesus covers me.

(Prayer for ancestral deeds)

9. Abba Father, I repent on behalf of my ancestors iniquity that brought curses into the bloodline and cry for the mercy of God in the name of Jesus.

10. Whatever the ancestors did for their health, wealth or fame that brought curses and misfortunes to the bloodline; I plead the blood of Jesus to cleanse it in the name of Jesus.

11. I renounce and denounce the ancestral covenants that stoke and fuel curses to operate in my bloodline in the name of Jesus

12. By the Power in the Blood Of Jesus, I cancel every covenant I have as a result of what my ancestors did on any evil Altar.

13. Any evil foundations from my ancestors speaking against me I mute your voice in Jesus' name.

14. By fire by thunder, I disconnect myself from my evil foundation in Jesus' name.

15. Wherever my umbilical cord has been buried for ancestral rituals, catch fire in Jesus' name.

16. By the anointing of God I cancel and nullify the oaths and vows that my forefathers made with demonic altars and cancel them in the name of Jesus.

17. Today in the name of Jesus I take captive of any family law that regulate, control and enforce poverty in the family. By fire by force I break and violate the law in the mighty name of Jesus.

18. I take captive of any family member-pouring libation to perpetuate the family trends of misfortunes that hold me in bondage and break out in the name of Jesus.

19. Henceforth, I reject, deject and refuse to follow any family law that keeps me in demonic bondage. I am coming out of family curses and break out in the name of Jesus.

20. I refuse to follow the family law that dictates what to eat and what not to eat. I violate the family law that states whom to marry and what to do- I reject it in the name of Jesus.

21. I take captive of the familiar spirit monitoring my life to ensure that I am part of the family curse and release fire in the name of Jesus.

22. Any evil activities of household witchcraft, sponsoring evil to the family members your time is up. Fire of God burn and destroy them in Jesus' name.

23. By fire by force I come against the demonic attacks programmed against my life. Curses and jinx I command you to backfire and return to sender in Jesus' name

24. I terminate any spell released into my bloodline that is causing unreasonable behaviours, rebellion and cancel its effects in Jesus' name.

25. The Lord is powerful and mighty in battle; I deploy the arrows of deliverance to my ancestral home and break the family curses in the mighty name of Jesus.

26. Any family law that sponsor evil occurrences and perpetual bondage receive fire. Holy Ghost terminate and consume the effects in the name of Jesus.

27. By the anointing of Holy Ghost I renounce and denounce the family laws and refuse to honour them. I cancel and terminate the operations of the family laws in the mighty name of Jesus.

28. Father, as I pray, cancel and break all the covenants that my ancestors established with demon gods. Let your wrath strike and destroy the evil altars in Jesus' name.

29. My forefathers who worshipped idols are dead and gone. I refuse to be a recipient of any repercussions of the idol worship I break out in Jesus' name.

30. Blood of Jesus cleanse me from the effects of the ancestral dedications and set me free. Let the power of God dedicate me to the altar of Jehovah God in the name of Jesus.

31. Father I pray, let the blood of Jesus wipe away the tribal marks, incisions, indentations and scratches that identify me with the family strongman in the name of Jesus.

32. By my will I renounce, denounce and reject the family laws that forbid certain activities on a certain day. I rebuke the spirit of witchcraft sponsoring the evil laws and cast it out in Jesus' name.

(Prayer for annulling evil contacts)

33. By the power in the blood of Jesus, as a result of my personal mistakes, may fire consume every contact from an evil altar in the name of Jesus.

34. By the power in the blood of Jesus, I redeem myself from any form of fellowship with evil altars.

35. I invoke the blood of Jesus to cleanse me and break the effects of bloodline curses afflicting my life in the name of Jesus.

36. By the power in the blood of Jesus, I redeem my mind from images and pictures the devil will show me, in Jesus' name.

37. By fire by thunder, every past event that has brought a plaque on me, die in Jesus' name.

38. Anything I have lost as a result of my past, I recover all in Jesus' name.

39. Every yoke that was assigned as a result of my past, break by fire by thunder in the name of Jesus.

40. By the power in the blood of Jesus, I purge every objects and concoctions I have swallow to come out, in the name of Jesus.

41. Today, by the force in the Blood Of Jesus, I redeem myself from any evil powers in Jesus' name.

42. Anything that has contaminated my life, die by fire.

43. In the name of Jesus, I renounce any charm, tokens, talisman, objects and concoctions from evil altars in the name of Jesus.

44. Restore unto me what the devil has stolen from me as a result of my past in Jesus' name.

(Prayers for deliverance)

45. In the name of Jesus, every generational curse, receive fire in Jesus' name.

46. By fire by thunder, any diminished cycle against my life, die.

47. By fire by thunder, any set back, die in Jesus' name.

48. In the name of Jesus, any struggle in my life, come to an end now.

49. Any evil power that is pressing me down, die by fire.

50. Any strong man from my father's house, from my mother's house, receive fire in Jesus' name.

51. Any satanic agent assigned to monitor my progress, die by fire.

52. Any monitoring spirit from my father's house, may fire locate you in Jesus' name.

53. Any monitoring spirit from my mother's house, may fire locate you in Jesus' name.

54. Any satanic delay in my life, die by fire.

55. Any opportunity aborters, who want to abort my visions, die by fire.

56. Let the power in the blood of Jesus be activated to flow into my foundation and break the stronghold of witchcraft manipulations in Jesus' name.

57. By the anointing that breaks the yoke I come against the enchantment, bewitchment and witchcraft manipulations that established curses in my family and break it in the name of Jesus.

58. Any altar receiving sacrifices to sponsor curses against my family the blood of Jesus is against you. Blood of Jesus silence the voice of evil sacrifice and speak for me in the mighty name of Jesus.

59. By the efficacy of the blood of Jesus I command an end to all torment and frustration of demonic attacks in my life in the Mighty name of Jesus.

60. Today I cancel the curses that bring chronic diseases, sickness and malaise into my bloodline. Blood of Jesus cleanse my bloodline in the name of Jesus.

61. My Lord Jesus Christ took my sickness, by His stripes I am healed, I break the bondage of diseases running through my family in Jesus' Name.

62. The Lord has blessed me and no one can curse me hallelujah! I command the power of God to strike dead anyone releasing incantations against me in Jesus' name.

63. Power of God cancel and erase the effects of evil arrows shot against me. By the anointing of God I command the evil arrows return to sender a hundredfold in the mighty name of Jesus.

64. Father I pray, let your power disconnect me from the village altars that I was initiated during festivals and cultural ritual participations in Jesus' name.

(Prayers for upliftment)

65. In the name of Jesus, any hidden treasures buried in secret altars, come forth now in Jesus' name.

66. My Father, my Father, let oil of favour locate me, right now in Jesus' name.

67. My Father, my Father, let the anointing to attract favour locate me now in Jesus' name.

68. In the name of Jesus, wherever my destiny helper is, may he/she locate me now in Jesus' name.

69. Anointing for victory, fall upon me right now in Jesus' name.

70. My father, my father may you enlarge my territory in Jesus' name.

71. My Father, Father, may Your mighty hand be upon me right now in Jesus' name.

72. My Father, my Father, may you keep me from evil so that I will not cause pain to others in Jesus' name.

73. My Father, my Father, give me Your glory that can not be doubted in the name of Jesus.

74. In the name of Jesus, Father give me the victory that cannot be disputed.

(Prayers for destroying evil works)

75. By fire by thunder, any enchantment from any evil altar, die in Jesus' name.

76. By fire by thunder, any divination emanated from evil altars, die in Jesus' name.

77. By fire by thunder, any evil pronouncements from witches and wizards from my ancestral home catch fire in Jesus' name.

78. Wherever my name, pictures and any objects belonging to me has been placed on evil altar, catch fire in Jesus' name.

79. Whenever they gather in their coven and my name is mention may the fire of God locate their coven in Jesus' name.

80. Any evil finger pointed at me in acquisition, may it wither in the name of Jesus.

81. Holy Ghost fire, consume and destroy the family strongman enforcing family laws to keep the family in perpetual bondage in the name of Jesus.

82. By the power of God, I command fire to burn and destroy all the witchcraft programming against my life in the name of Jesus.

83. Blood of Jesus cleanse me from the effects of festival food that I ate and flush out the point of contact. Let the blood of Jesus erase the remnants and make me whole in the name of Jesus.

84. Power of God, arrest and strike dead any witch or wizard projecting as animals to attack me in my dreams. Let them die before they turn back into humans in the name of Jesus.

85. By the finger of God I take captive of evil projections and cancel them. Holy Ghost fire, break, destroy and roast them to cinders in the name of Jesus.

86. By the anointing of the Living God, I come against the spirit of failure retrogression and near success syndrome and terminate the assignments in the name of Jesus.

87. By the efficacy of the blood of Jesus I cancel and negate the effect of witchcraft manipulations to waste youthful years in the family in Jesus' name.

88. By fire by force I enforce my liberty from the delegated strongman assigned to destroy marriages in the family in the mighty name of Jesus.

89. Any demonic siege militating against my marital glory I terminate your assignment and fire you to oblivion in the mighty name of Jesus' Christ of Nazareth.

90. I take captive of the powers assigned to cause marital distress in my bloodline; I terminate their agenda right now and scupper their evil plans in Jesus' name.

(Prayer for Health)

91. Witches, wizards, sorcerers, eaters of flesh or drinkers of blood operating in my family receive fire. I shut down every supply and command them to drink their own blood and eat their own flesh in Jesus' name.

92. Today in the name of Jesus I put an end to the captivity of my virtues and command the bloodthirsty demons and witchcraft agents to release my virtues now in Jesus' name.

93. I superimpose the power of God against the unknown and cancel any impending danger programmed against my spouse, offspring and siblings in the mighty name of Jesus.

94. I invoke the blood of Jesus to purge my organs and the entire body of any pollution caused by family witchcraft. Spirit of God infuse me with new lease of life in the name of Jesus.

95. By the Blood of Jesus I overhaul my system to eject demonic deposits by witchcraft devices. I negate the effects of household witchcraft and cancel them from my life in the name of Jesus.

96. The blessings of the Lord are my portion; I plead the blood of Jesus to cleanse and erase the bloodline curses and eradicate them in the name of Jesus.

97. By the death and resurrection of Jesus Christ I inherited eternal life. Satan, you did not die for my salvation, so I refuse to inherit your evil law it is null and void in the name of Jesus.

98. Abba Father who brings life to the dead revive any aspect of my life that is dead. Holy Spirit energise and fill me with your fire in the name of Jesus.

99. My Lord Jesus Christ is the Bread of Life hallelujah! By the death and resurrection of Jesus Christ I cancel the family covenant of death in the name of Jesus.

100. The curse of the Lord is in the house of the wicked. By the finger of God I deploy the blood of Jesus to break the yoke of bondage and cancels the effects of wickedness in Jesus' name.

101. I take authority and come against the impending dangers as a result of promises, vows and oaths made to demonic gods. I cancel the agreements that mortgaged the family to the devil in Jesus' name.

102. I superimpose the power of God against idol worship, ancestral worship and occult involvement. Power of God, break the yoke and set me free in the name of Jesus.

<h1 style="text-align:center">(Prayer against family altars and witchcrafts)</h1>

103.   I am the redeemed of the Lord I come against the power behind the scene that regulate and sponsor family laws and cancel them in the mighty name of Jesus.

104.   I am the battle-axe of the Lord hallelujah! The Lord has trained my hands for battle; I batter and strangle the household witchcraft and demolish their coven in Jesus' name.

105.   Holy Ghost fire break and destroy the demonic altars that sponsor the evil family laws and break them. Fire of God consume the shrines and satanic altars in the name of Jesus.

106.   I stand in the righteousness of Christ and enter my ancestral home to demolish the altars, totems, tokens and set alight the demonic devices in the mighty name of Jesus.

107.   I rebuke the spirit of divination operating in my bloodline. Power of God locate the satanic oracles in the family and strike them dead in the name of Jesus.

108.   Today in the name of Jesus I take authority and come against household witchcraft and fire it. Any witchcraft manipulations to bewitch the family receive fire in the name of Jesus.

109.   Any member of the family sponsoring witchcraft manipulations by sacrifices, divination, incantations and pouring libation thunder of God strike them dead in the name of Jesus.

110.   Whosoever has allowed themselves to be used as the custodian of the witchcraft in the family Holy Ghost fire strike them dead in the mighty name of Jesus'.

111.   Anyone pouring libation and sacrificing animals to reconcile the family to the ancestral worship receive fire. Power of God, remove my name from the ancestry register and set me free in Jesus' name.

112.   Whoever is sitting at their altar releasing incantations to curse me and bring calamity to the family fall down and die in the mighty name of Jesus

113.   By the anointing of God I cancel the law of premature deaths in all aspects of my life and speak life in all my endeavours in the mighty name of Jesus.

114.   By the power of the Living God I break the family law of sickness, infirmity, sickness that defy medical therapy and speak healing, restoration and revival in the mighty name of Jesus.

115.   I take authority and come against the witches and wizards in my sphere of influence and fire them. Holy Ghost strike and destroy the unfriendly friends stabbing me at the back in Jesus' name.

116. Anyone smiling at me while plotting and scheming behind my back receive fire. Holy Ghost fire locate them and remove them from my vicinity in the name of Jesus.

117. Father I pray anyone plotting and scheming to bring my ministry down remove them by divine subtraction. Power of God locate and attract my divine helpers in the name of Jesus.

(Prayer for declaration)

118. Let the Prince of Peace bring peace in every aspect of my life. The shalom of God prevail in my household and overwhelm us with peace in the name of Jesus.

119. I speak long life for my children they will be fruitful in all aspects of life. Their dwelling will be fertile like the Garden of Eden in the mighty name of Jesus.

120. I prophesy that my children will excel and wax great in all aspects of life. The grace of God is upon my children the blessing of God will overtake them in the name of Jesus.

121. The Lord has delivered me and elevated me to a higher paradigm. The shackles of family bondage are broken and I am free from the yoke of family witchcraft in the name of Jesus.

122. The arrows of deliverance have set me free from the fetters of family law. Henceforth I use the blood of Jesus to enact godly laws of righteousness in the name of Jesus.

123. Jehovah you are God of restoration, bring restoration to my family, revive our fortunes and bring restitution into the life of our family in the mighty name of Jesus.

124. I speak divine acceleration for my seed stagnation shall never enter their vicinity. Goodness and mercy shall follow my children all the days of their lives in the name of Jesus.

125. The Lord has delivered me from the bounds of bondage, captivity and demonic servitude hallelujah. Henceforth as for me and my house we shall serve the Lord in the mighty name of Jesus.

126. The Lord who answers by fire has delivered me from the stronghold of household witchcraft. I am matching forward to my promised land in the name of Jesus.

127.   Let God arise and the enemy scatter, when the enemy comes after me, my Father will raise a standard against it.

128.   The Lord is my shepherd I will not want; goodness and mercy shall follow me all days of my life in the name of Jesus.

129.   Oh Lord, grant me the grace to overcome my old self and to obey your principles and ordinances in Jesus' name.

130.   Oh Lord, may Your Holy Ghost Power empower me to overcome my past in Jesus' name.

131.   Thank you Lord for answering my prayers; thank you Lord for breathing life into the dead situation. Thank you Lord for lifting me from the sinking sand in Jesus' name.

132.   Thank you Lord for bringing deliverance to my household and setting me free. I seal my deliverance with the blood of Jesus in the mighty name of Jesus'.

133.   I believe I'm a new creature in Christ, I don't owe the devil anything in Jesus' name.

134.   I'm now on fire for the Lord, in Jesus' name, Amen!

Contact information

Phone: +31 -653383185

Email: pastorquaysonkay@outlook.com

Facebook: Quayson Kay